RIPON CATHEDRAL

CANON W. E. WILKINSON, B.A.

THE Cathedral Church of S. Peter and S. Wilfrid at Ripon stands on ground which has been used for 1,300 years as a place of Christian worship. Her Saxon crypt, one of the oldest buildings in England, was part of the first church to be raised on this site, and it links us across the centuries with our heathen forefathers. This church, probably the first stone church in the north of England, was built by Wilfrid, a famous Christian leader of the 7th century. Wilfrid's younger contemporary Bede, the monk historian of Jarrow, describes how a little monastery (or mission station) was planted in the heathen village of

*   *   *

FACING PAGE: *The Cathedral from the East.*

ABOVE: *The Cathedral from the South-East.*

Rhypum about A.D. 655, and how Wilfrid, its second Abbot, enlarged this monastery, built a great church, and became a distinguished statesman-bishop in the huge kingdom of Northumbria. Ripon monastery, which disappeared at the time of the Danish invasions, is still remembered in Holland for Wilfrid's celebrated pupil Willibrord, the missionary to the Low Countries, who became Archbishop of Utrecht in A.D. 696.

Wilfrid ruled the church in Northumbria for many years as Bishop of York, wielding supreme power, though the title of Archbishop was not used until some years after his death; but he made his home in Ripon, and here he built a magnificent church, which was regarded by his contemporaries as one of the finest buildings west of the Alps. As this church was destroyed, except for the Crypt, by the Danes two hundred years later, we cannot be sure

what it was like; but Wilfrid certainly modelled it on the churches that he had seen and admired in Rome, which were of the basilica type with pillars and side aisles, and contained many gaily coloured pictures and figures of the apostles and saints. Wilfrid's church was probably about one-third the size of our present Minster, and the Crypt lay under the High Altar. It is recorded that the altar hangings were of purple and gold, and that Wilfrid gave to his new church the text of the Four Gospels "written out in letters of gold on purple parchment, and illuminated". Wilfrid loved the grandeur and dignity of Roman ways, and the goal of his long life (634–709) was to bring the English Church under the Roman obedience.

The Crypt of this celebrated Saxon church has survived into the 20th century, and every year hundreds of people go down the narrow medieval

1

The West Prospect of ye Church of Rippon.

Ripponensis eccl: facies occidentalis.

staircase to visit it. The little stone room is empty now, but in Wilfrid's day it contained the caskets of sacred relics (bones or objects associated with the saints) which he had brought back from Rome to be used in the dedication of his new churches. A medieval super-stition about Wilfrid's Needle, a narrow hole on the north side of the Crypt, has persisted so long that it ought to be mentioned here. The ability to crawl through the hole from the Crypt into the passage outside was supposed to be a proof of chastity. There is little doubt that the legend was inspired by the practice of trial by ordeal. Ripon Minster was granted the right of Sanctuary by King Athelstan in A.D. 934, and also the right to try the accused man in a church court, where he was submitted to trial by ordeal of fire and water. Sanctuary was offered within a mile of the church, and one of the boundary crosses still remains at Sharow.

Wilfrid received munificent gifts from successive Northumbrian kings, and owned and administered immense properties around Ripon. Later Arch-bishops of York inherited these pos-sessions and privileges, and main-tained down the centuries the close connection between York and Ripon. Many Archbishops of York come into this story as benefactors of Ripon Minster. Until Bishopthorpe Palace, within a few miles of York, was built in 1220, the episcopal palace in Ripon, with its extensive deer-park, was a favourite country residence of the archbishops. This palace stood on the site of the present Court House north west of the Minster.

Wilfrid's name and fame have re-mained dear to the citizens of Ripon. In the dedication of the 12th-century church, his name was added to that of

Continued on page 4

*   *   *

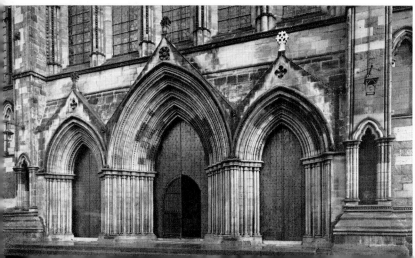

ABOVE: *A 17th-century print of the West Front of Ripon Cathedral. The spires were removed as a precautionary measure in 1664 after the fall of the spire on the Central Tower in 1660.*

LEFT: *The porches of the Early English West Front. The oak doors date from 1673. Visitors will see this date patterned in nails on the middle door.*

FACING PAGE: *The austere West Front was built by Walter de Grey, Arch-bishop of York 1215–1256. The bells are situated in the South-West Tower.*

2

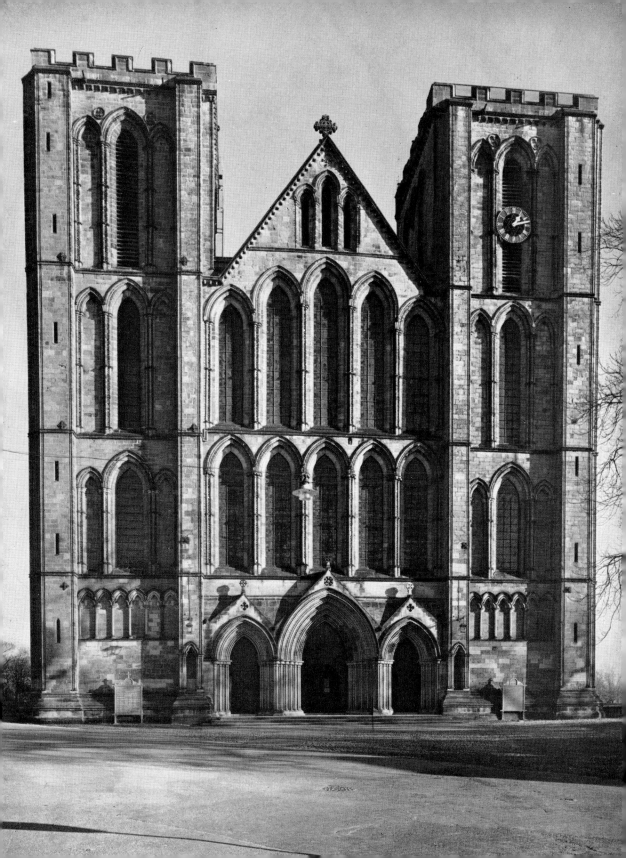

St. Peter, and his shrine in the Minster was a popular place of pilgrimage all through the Middle Ages. Today the people of Ripon honour his memory every year during the first week in August. On Saturday a citizen dressed as a Saxon bishop rides through the town on a gaily caparisoned white horse; on Sunday Wilfrid is specially remembered at all Cathedral services.

Ripon, with the rest of Yorkshire, suffered terrible devastation, first by the Danes, who destroyed Wilfrid's church and monastery in the 9th century, and then by the Normans who laid waste a second church built on the same site. After the Battle of Hastings our northern ancestors proved rebellious, and William the Conqueror swore "by the splendour of God" that he would not leave one living soul north of the Humber. The harrying of the north in 1069 was a brutal operation, and when Domesday Book was compiled seventeen years later, large areas of Yorkshire were described as derelict and uninhabited.

But the Normans were enthusiastic builders, and a third church soon rose on the ruin left by the Conqueror's soldiers. Probably the patron of this church was Thomas of Bayeux, the first Norman Archbishop of York, who spent a good deal of time in Ripon, and died here. Two examples of early Norman work which formed part of this church are incorporated into our present building: the apsidal chapel at the east end of the Chapter House, and the vaulted Norman Undercroft below it. The Undercroft has recently been converted partly into a mortuary chapel, the Chapel of All Souls, and partly into a choir rehearsal and robing room. The south wall of the Chapter House, which was also part of the third church, has lately needed extensive repairs, and these repairs have restored the Chapter House as an aisle of the Norman church with its lovely apsidal sanctuary.

In this church, Archbishop Thurstan and the monks from St. Mary's Abbey, York, worshipped on Christmas Day 1132, the day before they tramped up Skelldale to found Fountains Abbey. Thurstan, like his predecessors, spent a good deal of time in his episcopal palace at Ripon, and, as Lord of the Manor of the whole district, he was able to present a piece of his own land to the Fountains monks.

We now come to the great builder of the fourth church, Archbishop Roger Pont l'Eveque (1154–1181). He holds his place in English history for the support he gave to King Henry II in

Continued on page 6

*   *   *

ABOVE (left): *This handsome pulpit of beaten metal on marble columns was made c. 1900. The beautifully modelled figures represent four Saxon Saints.*

ABOVE (right): *Hugh Ripley, last Wakeman and first Mayor of Ripon, died 1637. The monument was put up in 1637, defaced in 1643, and restored in 1730.*

FACING PAGE: *This view of the Nave, looking East, shows the most remarkable feature of Ripon Cathedral, a central tower with two round and two pointed arches. On the right of the 12th-century arch we see where the 16th-century builders began to convert it into a pointed arch like the one over the organ.*

his quarrel with Archbishop Thomas Becket of Canterbury; but in Ripon he is remembered and honoured as the patron and architect of our present Cathedral. Roger's work in Ripon Minster provides one of the finest surviving examples of Norman transitional building, i.e., the transition from the round to the pointed arch.

The Nave of Roger's church had no side aisles, and the windows were few and high; but we can picture it in imagination because two of the original bays remain at the west end, and portions of the original wall are visible at the east end of the present Nave. Probably the plain lower walls of the narrow, dimly-lit Nave were covered with gaily-coloured frescoes. Some early painting may still be seen on the left-hand wall as we climb the stairs from the South Transept to the present Library. There was, of course, no seating in a medieval nave: the weak went to the wall, where a stone seat was usually provided.

The North Transept remains as Roger built it, and also part of the north side of the Choir. His Choir had the unusual feature of side aisles. He incorporated part of the earlier church, as we have already seen, into his new Chapter House, building port-hole windows into the old wall, and adding the vaulted roof. Except for the addition of nave aisles, the plan of our present Cathedral is almost that of Archbishop Roger.

The Archbishop gave £1,000 to the building fund, a huge sum in those days; but the revenues of York were immense in medieval times. The building was begun in 1154, but in 1181, the year of Roger's death, appeals for more money were still being launched by the Chapter, and "all humble Christian folk" were exhorted "for the love of God and of St. Wilfrid" to give generously. Subscribers were promised, "as long as they lived a mass would be sung for them every day, and when they departed this life, another mass would be celebrated for their souls, and for the souls of all their parents, in relief of the penalties of their sins".

The next important building operation was undertaken by Archbishop Walter de Grey of York in 1220. He built the present Early English West Front with its twin towers. The towers were crowned with wooden spires covered with lead. The West Front evidently took many years to complete, because thirty-eight years later

Continued on page 8

FACING PAGE (above): *The South aisle was added to the 12th-century Nave in 1502. The Tudor font in the foreground has replaced a Norman font now in the South-West Tower. The altar tomb on the right has the famous carving of the Ripon lion seen on page 22.*

FACING PAGE (below left): *The Saxon crypt was built by St. Wilfred in 672 under the high altar of his great church. The hole on the left of the photograph is called St. Wilfred's Needle.*

FACING PAGE (below right): *This fine pulpit was removed from above the Screen to make room for an enlarged organ. Part of the rather flamboyant 18th-century tomb of Sir Thomas Blackett is seen on left of the picture.*

ABOVE: *Visitors will take particular note of the splendid clerestory windows built early in the 16th century when the Nave was enlarged. The statue of James I stands on a pillar under the Central Tower.*

ABOVE (right): *The ceiling of the North Transept has been recently restored and re-gilded. The figures over the door into the South Choir aisle are a memorial to Dean Owen, who died in 1940.*

RIGHT: *A perfect example of Norman Transitional building, the Markenfield Chapel contains the 14th-century tomb of Sir Thomas Markenfield, and a 15th-century Markenfield tomb can also be seen outside the Chapel.*

7

the Pope issued a bull granting indulgences of 100 days to all who subscribed to Ripon fabric fund. Archbishop de Grey also built the South Transept of York Minster, and the episcopal palace at Bishopthorpe, which was to bring to an end the Archbishops' practice of using Ripon as a country residence. Another of his benefactions to Ripon was the foundation of a seventh prebend (that of Stanwick) which added another canon to the Chapter of the Minster.

By the time of the Norman Conquest in 1066, Ripon Minster, the monasterium of Wilfrid's day, had become a College of secular canons, or prebendaries. The other six prebends from which the canons derived their independent incomes were Monkton, Givendale, Sharow, Nunwick, Studley and Thorpe. All these places had been presented to the College by different Archbishops of York, and formed part of the huge parish of Ripon. The canonries remained in the gift of the Archbishop, but the parish was a Peculiar over which the Chapter ruled. Ripon Minster continued to be one of the three mother churches in the diocese of York; the other two were Beverley and Southwell.

Evidently the seven canons did not always take their duties seriously, as we find Archbishop Romanus of York (1286–1298) reproaching them for not living in Ripon, and failing to take part in the daily services. They were also neglecting the music. The non-residence of the secular canons seems to have been a continuing abuse in the 13th and 14th centuries. Some of the canons simply drew their incomes and put in underpaid vicars (substitutes), while others were not religious men at all, but were appointed by King or Archbishop as a reward for secular services. During these years of slackness, the fabric of the Minster was obviously neglected, because the next important alteration was caused by the dangerous state of the Choir.

In 1286, Archbishop Romanus embarked on the rebuilding of the eastern part of the Choir, and ordered each canon to contribute a tenth part of the income of his prebend until the restoration was completed. Indulgences were offered to other subscribers to the fabric fund. The Choir was restored in the elaborate Decorated style, and our great East Window was constructed. It remains today one of the largest and finest examples of geometrical tracery in the country. The

present glass dates from the 19th century, and is not worthy of its noble frame. The fine painted stone bosses in the Choir roof are thought to date from this period; one particularly attractive carving represents the angel driving Adam and Eve out of the Garden of Eden.

The early part of the 14th century was a troubled time for the whole of the north of England. After their great victory at Bannockburn over King Edward II's army in 1314, the Scots were continually raiding the northern counties, and in 1318 they reached Ripon, having plundered Northaller-

Continued on page 10

★   ★   ★

ABOVE: *The Choir Screen was erected c. 1500. The present angel choir and the large figures below (illustrated on the left) date from 1947. Saint Willibrord (above), a pupil of Saint Wilfrid, who became Archbishop of Utrecht.*

FACING PAGE: *References to an organ are found in the Ripon Registers as early as 1399. The present organ was built in 1878 and extensively restored in 1912, 1950 and 1963. The organ case was designed by Sir Gilbert Scott in 1860.*

ton and Boroughbridge. The inhabitants fled to the Minster, which they fortified and held for three days. On payment of a ransom the invaders withdrew, but returned the following year and did considerable damage to the Minster. Certain repairs were carried out, but the middle years of the 14th century brought the scourge of the Black Death to England, from which almost half the population perished.

Towards the end of the century, Ripon recovered her prosperity, and probably about this time the Lady Chapel, now used as a Cathedral Library, was built over the Chapter House. The style of the architecture is late Decorated. The position of the Lady Loft, upstairs on the south side of the Choir, is very unusual. Most cathedral Lady Chapels are placed behind the high altar at the east end, but at Ripon Minster the steep fall of the ground makes any extension eastwards very difficult. Another possible explanation is that the shrine of St. Wilfrid, a popular place of pilgrimage until the Reformation, monopolised the east end of the Minster. This shrine lay under the East window. St. Wilfrid's Chapel is used today for the daily celebrations of Holy Communion.

The first fifty years of the 15th century were again marked by indolence and neglect on the part of the canonical body, and about 1450 a major calamity befell Ripon Minster. The south-east corner of the Central Tower collapsed. For some years the Minster was unusable, and services were held in the Lady Kirk, a chapel in St. Mary's Gate, of which no trace survives today.

It was no time to embark on extensive repairs, for the horizon was

Continued on page 16

★   ★   ★

ABOVE and LEFT: *The windows in the picture above show clearly the break between the 12th-century Norman Transitional work of Archbishop Roger on the left and the early Decorated work of the late 13th century on the right. The joining of the old to the new is marked by carvings of three grotesque faces seen at the left.*

FACING PAGE: *This splendid window is one of the finest examples of Geometrical tracery in England. It is over 50 feet high and 25 feet wide. Note the bosses in the roof, illustrated on page 14.*

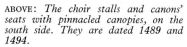

ABOVE: *The choir stalls and canons' seats with pinnacled canopies, on the south side. They are dated 1489 and 1494.*

EXTREME LEFT: *Bench end of the Bishop's throne showing a fighting elephant and a centaur with axe and shield.*

BELOW (extreme left): *Bench end of the Mayor's stall. Traditionally, every Mayor of Ripon is installed here by the Dean at the start of his year of office.*

LEFT (above and below): *Samson carrying off the gates of Gaza; a fox running away with a goose between a lady holding a distaff and a hound. These are two of the 34 beautifully carved miserere seats that were carved c. 1490 by Ripon craftsmen and are among the glories of Ripon Minster.*

★

FACING PAGE: *View of the Chancel looking west from the High Altar.*

ABOVE: *The reredos is a memorial to the Ripon men who fell in the 1914-18 war. It was designed by Sir Ninian Comper and represents Northumbrian saints and leaders of the 7th century. On the wall behind are figures of St. Peter and St. Wilfrid, patron saints of Ripon Cathedral.*

*

LEFT: *The stone bosses in the ceiling of the Choir date from about 1300. These pictures show Adam and Eve and two ecclesiastical figures.*

*

FACING PAGE: *This picture shows an organist's seat, over the Chancel entrance, supported by a fine carving of the Trinity. The carved hand, for beating time, can still be moved.*

14

darkened by the prospect of civil war. The rule of a weak King, Henry VI, and his unscrupulous Queen, had brought anarchy to the country and led to the outbreak of the Wars of the Roses. Ripon went unscathed, but the bloody battles of Wakefield and Towton were fought less than forty miles away, and there must have been fear and uncertainty in every heart. Peace and stability gradually returned after the accession of the first Tudor king, Henry VII, in 1485, and the most ambitious building programme to be undertaken since the 12th century was carried out during the next fifty years. It included the rebuilding of the south side of the Choir, and of the east side of the South Transept, and also the great project of enlarging the Nave.

The rebuilding of the Central Tower was never finished, and this failure of the 15th-century builders to complete their task has given our Minster one of its most unusual features, a tower with two rounded and two pointed arches. The south and east sides are in the Perpendicular style of the 15th century, while the north and west sides remain in the Norman Transitional style of the 12th century. An observant visitor, looking towards the crossing from the west end, must immediately be struck by the curious appearance of the central arch.

The collapse of the tower destroyed the screen, and did considerable damage to the west end of the Choir and to the South Transept. The present Perpendicular screen dates from this period of restoration. All the figures in the niches are new, 20th cen-

Continued on page 18

★   ★   ★

ABOVE: *The Chapter House, originally part of the first Norman Church (1080) was converted into a Chapter House by Archbishop Roger. Considerable restoration was carried out by Sir Albert Richardson in 1956.*

LEFT: *The lovely apsidal chapel at the east end of the Chapter House dates from the 11th century. The spiral staircase on the left of the photograph goes up to the Lady Loft.*

FACING PAGE: *The staircase in the South Transept leads up to the Lady Chapel or Lady Loft, which is now used as the Library. The Mallorie Chapel is on the right of the stairs. Against the south wall is an 18th-century bust by Nollekens of William Waddell of Newby Hall.*

tury, except the lovely little representation of God the Father in the hood of the archway.

There seems no doubt that there was an organ on the old screen. In the accounts for 1399 "the leather of two horse-skins for two new pairs of bellows for the organ" cost 2s. 8d. In 1453, Will Organmaker was paid 20s. for "mending the organs". In 1695 a new organ was built, "one of the sweetest-toned in the kingdom"; another in 1834, and the present organ in 1878. A little gallery projects on the chancel side of the screen, and a carved wooden hand, once used to beat time, can still be worked by a lever.

The beautiful Choir Stalls were begun in 1489 and completed within five years. Some of the canopies were destroyed in 1660 by the fall of the spire above the Central Tower, but skilful copies have replaced them, and today only an expert can distinguish the original 15th-century work from that of their 19th-century copies. The Misericords and bench-ends provide exquisite and amusing examples of medieval craftsmanship. As the underneath part of the seat was not much in evidence, the woodcarvers were allowed plenty of freedom in their choice of subjects; these are by no means all sacred, and often grotesque and fantastic. The thirty-four misericords at Ripon all have different carved pictures, set in lovely conventional flower designs. Under the Bishop's throne, Caleb and Joshua are carrying the grapes, watched by a headless body and a bodiless head; another has Samson carrying the gates of Gaza; a third has Jonah coming out of the whale's mouth; a fourth has a pelican feeding her young; a fifth has two pigs dancing to bagpipes played by a third pig. Other seats have dragons and foxes, and all of them are beautifully designed and skilfully carved. The Ripon woodcarvers were renowned craftsmen; they also carved the choir stalls at Beverley Minster, Bridlington Priory and Manchester Cathedral. It is recorded in the Minster Fabric Rolls that the chief craftsman was called William Brownflet, later known as William Carver, and that he was paid for his work at the rate of 6d. a day.

The Choir Stalls were finished in 1494, and about this time the rebuilding of the Nave began. There is a suggestion that the 12th-century Nave had fallen into disrepair "through age and storms and neglect"—the recurring reason for restoration appeals; but probably the restorers thought Archbishop Roger's Nave too narrow, dark, and old-fashioned for so important a church, and so they determined to transform it into a splendid Perpendicular Nave. It remains today one of the widest and loveliest, as it is also one of the latest, of Perpendicular Naves.

The south aisle was begun in 1502, the north aisle in 1515, and the work was almost finished when the Tudor antiquary Leland visited Ripon in 1538. But the Nave aisles were not yet stone-vaulted when the Reformation put an end to all building projects, and they were roofed in wood until the 19th century. It is recorded that two Archbishops of York and all the canons

Continued on page 22

FACING PAGE: *Cases of early printed books, both English and foreign, in the Cathedral Library. Many date from before 1500.*

ABOVE: *The Resurrection (top) and the Coronation of the Virgin are carvings in alabaster that were formerly part of the decorations in the medieval Minster.*

RIGHT: *The East Window of the library with the arms of the local gentry and bishops. An extremely rare 12th-century manuscript Bible lies on the table—one of the library's precious manuscript books, the earliest of which is a pre-Conquest fragment.*

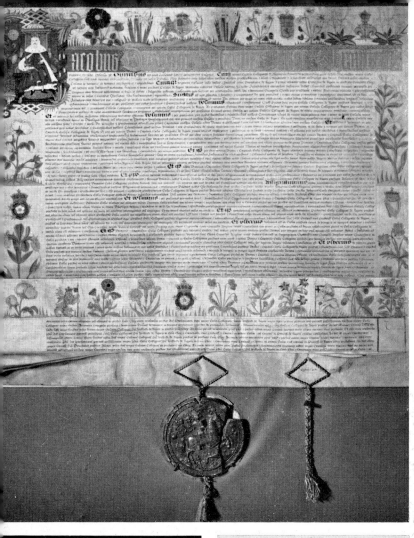

LEFT: *This colourful charter, with the great seal of James I attached, records the reconstitution of the Ripon Charter in 1604, and the restoration of the revenues sequestrated in 1545.*

ABOVE: *A page of the 13th-century manuscript Bible, showing four illuminated capitals. This book, written on vellum, is an exquisite example of early medieval penmanship.*

BELOW (extreme left): *A tract on the Old Testament, beautifully printed by Koburger of Nuremburg in 1490. This book once belonged to Fountains Abbey, as can be seen from the note at the top of the page.*

LEFT: *A page from a copy of the first English Prayer Book of 1549.*

★

FACING PAGE: *The West window is an elder sister to the famous Five Sisters window in the North Transept of York Minster. Both were built by Archbishop Walter de Grey (1215-1256). The glass dates from 1886. This window is a memorial to Bishop Longley and Bishop Bickersteth.*

20

contributed to the building fund, and the usual indulgences, never again to be issued, were promised to the other subscribers. The last piece of work to be completed before the Reformation was the rebuilding of the three western-most bays on the south side of the Choir.

The break with Rome came in 1534, and King Henry VIII was declared to be the supreme head of the Church in England. The monasteries, including Fountains Abbey, were suppressed, and the shrines of the saints, including St. Wilfrid's shrine, were dismantled. It was the end of an epoch. For the next few years the affairs of Ripon Minster were managed by an intelligent and businesslike canon called Marmaduke Bradley. At the request of the King's Commissioners, Bradley had left Ripon to become the last Abbot of Fountains, and to negotiate her surrender to the Crown; but he had never given up his canonry, and after the Dissolution he returned to his duties at Ripon.

These were anxious years for wealthy corporations. The dissolution of the monasteries had yielded rich revenues to Henry VIII—the income of Fountains was £1,000—but he continued to be short of money, and in 1545 Parliament passed an Act conferring on him the property of all colleges, chantries,

hospitals and guilds. In 1547 the blow fell on Ripon Minster; the College of canons was dissolved, and all its possessions were annexed to the Duchy of Lancaster. A small sum from the confiscated revenue was reserved for the payment of a few lesser clergy to look after the large parish of Ripon. A staff of five vicars were doing this work during the reign of Elizabeth I.

In 1604 King James I re-established the canonical Chapter at Ripon, and restored part of her former revenues. The Charter of Restoration, a large and gaily illuminated document with the royal seal attached, is displayed today in the Chapter House. Under the new constitution, Ripon Minster was to be a Collegiate Church with a dean and six canons. Our great benefactor, James I, is honoured today by two statues in the Cathedral, one, presented by the York Chapter in 1811, high up on the north-west pillar of the Central Tower; another, of 20th-century workmanship, in the Screen

King James I also granted a new Charter to the city under which the old wakeman—watchman or head of the city council—became the first mayor. One of the servants of the wakeman was the hornblower, who blew his horn outside the wakeman's house and in the market place every evening at 9 p.m., when the Minster bell tolled

curfew. Curfew is still rung and the horn is still blown in Ripon today, a custom that has lasted for over 1,000 years. King James spent a night in Ripon on his way up to Scotland in 1617, and Dean Higgin, second Dean of Ripon, greeted him with a learned and flattering Latin speech, which was exactly to James' taste. He was also given by the city a pair of silver spurs, the manufacture of which was a new and prosperous industry.

Dean Higgin was an enthusiastic collector of books, and the founder of our considerable Library. The Cathedral Library, which is now housed in the Lady Loft, contains many treasures, including an unusually large number of early printed books. The manuscript books include a 12th-century copy of the Apocalypse and the Catholic Epistles, a beautifully

*　　*　　*

ABOVE: *This carving on an altar tomb in the South Nave aisle represents a grove of trees and a lion with a man kneeling. Part of a large monumental brass, it was made in a Flemish workshop in the 14th century. There is a tradition that the marble top was used by Ripon merchants for counting money when a business deal was being negotiated.*

illuminated Latin Bible dating from early in the 13th century, and a 15th-century York Psalter containing the Ripon Offices of St. Wilfrid. There is a perfect copy of the 1549 first Prayer Book in English.

Ripon became involved in the Civil War that broke out between King and Parliament in 1642, and the following year the town was occupied by Parliamentary troops. Soldiers forced their way into the Minster, and either from sheer indiscipline, or more probably, from a fanatical determination to destroy 'idolatrous images', they smashed most of the beautiful medieval glass, and some of the wall monuments. Some collected fragments of medieval glass may be seen today in the western-most window of the south aisle in the Nave.

The two principal actors in the tragic drama of the Civil War both came to Ripon. King Charles spent two nights here in 1646 as a prisoner on his journey south from Newcastle, and Oliver Cromwell paid two visits to the town. During the Commonwealth, the Chapter was again dissolved, and revived at the Restoration of Charles II in 1660.

In 1660 the spire of the Central Tower fell through the roof and wrecked several of the canopies in the Choir Stalls. The damage was repaired, but the spire was never rebuilt; and in 1664 the spires on the twin towers of the West Front were also removed.

The later history of Ripon Minster is mainly a story of restoration. An extensive repair of the roof was done in 1829 at a cost of £6,000; and a complete overhaul costing £40,000 was begun by Sir Gilbert Scott in 1862 and finished in 1870. Another overhaul, at an estimated cost of £150,000 is now being undertaken, under the direction of Sir Albert Richardson.

Five 20th-century monuments deserve to be mentioned here. The Nave pulpit, richly decorated in beaten metal, was given to the Cathedral in

Continued on page 24

*   *   *

ABOVE: *The Norman Undercroft beneath the Chapter House is now converted into a mortuary chapel through the generosity of the late Mr. George Chapman.*

RIGHT: *The Norman doorway into the South Transept was part of Archbishop Roger's 12th-century church.*

1913. The Reredos of the High Altar, depicting 7th-century saints, is a memorial to the men of Ripon who died in the 1914–1918 War. It is the work of Sir Ninian Comper. The figures in the niches of the Screen were presented by lovers of the Cathedral after the Second World War. The coloured figures above the entrance to the south Choir aisle were given as a memorial to Dean Owen, who died in 1940. The Chapel of the Holy Spirit in the south choir aisle was given by the family of the late Charles Crabtree and dedicated in 1970. It is a rugged metal creation, the work of Leslie Durbin.

In 1836 the Collegiate Church of Ripon, which had been for many centuries an important mother church within the diocese of York, became the Cathedral Church of the new diocese of Ripon.

The Minster today is both a Cathedral and a Parish Church. The daily offices are said or sung without intermission, and every year thousands of people from the diocese as well as from the city take part in Sunday and special services. Ripon Minster is still well attended and well loved, a perfect building in which to offer our imperfect prayers. Other men have laboured, and we enter into their labours. May other men enter into ours.

*　　*　　*

ABOVE: *This picture well contrasts the 12th century South Transept with the Nave and south wall of the Tower which was built three hundred years later.*

LEFT: *This Aerofilms photograph shows Ripon Cathedral standing today, as it has stood for 800 years, in the middle of a busy market town, a landmark of beauty for miles around. Perhaps it was more impressive three hundred years ago when tall spires crowned the squat towers, but nothing can alter its noble grandeur and solid simplicity.*

*　　*　　*

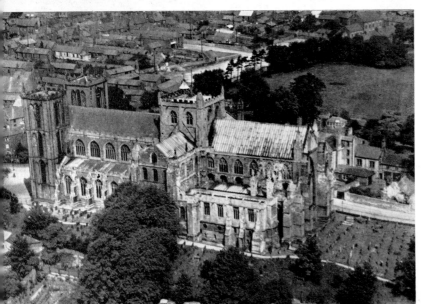

ACKNOWLEDGMENTS
The publishers are indebted to the Dean and Chapter of Ripon Cathedral for their co-operation in the production of this book. Except for the aerial view, *left*, and front cover picture, all the photographs are by A. F. Kersting, F.I.I.P., F.R.P.S.

SBN 85372 3   771/20